Stepping from Behind the Shadow

Johnnie Mae McCall

Stepping from Behind the Shadow

Johnnie Mae McCall

Unless otherwise notes, all scriptures are taken from The King James Version.

Published by "J Mae McCall & Co."

Printed in the United States of America

ISBN: 978--1-7369517-1-2

Dedication

Again, Jesus spoke to them, saying, "I'm the light of the world. Whoever follows me will not walk-in darkness but will have the light of life". John 8:12

I dedicate this book to my elder sister Patricia Pair. As she now appears from behind the shadow, beneath her feet, lay the chains that once held her locked behind the shadows of guilt in shame. Resiliency has become her portion as she continues to stand from behind the shadow. She now shows the world what it looks like to be liberated from the darkness of past trauma and abuse as she lives in the brilliance of the father's restoring power. Continue shining in his glory.

Table of Contents

Acknowledgments

~Thank You~

I would like to say thank you first to Yahweh, the giver and sustainer of life. Indeed, it is you that called all things into existence and caused all things to be. Apostle Cierra L. Jones, I thank God for your covering, prayers, and leadership. You are God's gift to my life, and your leadership is God-driven. Thank you for continually pushing me to move beyond. I can honestly say that I have matured and tap into a new frequency that has propelled me into maturity. You have graced my life and walked me through many deliverance levels, and I am thankful for this. Apostle Kirby Gant, I honor you, Prophetess Annie Jones; you have graced my life and instilled that "It is possible."

Bishop George Searight and Pastor Mary Searight thank you for your demonstration of pure leadership. Overseer Roderick Allen and Elder

Sheila D. Allen, you called a dead thing to life, and here I stand. Dr. James P, Williams, and the Faculty of the United Bible College I am that everyday learning pupil. Thank you for opening up to the world of theology.

To my family, thank you for believing and supporting me wholeheartedly. To my mother's, you know who you are. Mom Madison, Ma Vicky Villines, Ma Jones, and the others, I love you.

Finally, to all of you who thought it not robbery and decided to purchase a copy of this book, you are filled with the gift of potential.

Foreward

There are times that we find ourselves in a dark place, and because we have been there for such a long time, we become impervious to it. There is a way out, and sometimes God will send someone along to assist us in getting back into the place where he called us to be.

I am elated and honored to tell you about my friend, Johnnie Mae McCall. I have known her for six years, and she is the epitome of a Proverbs 31 Woman. She does not just talk it; she walks it. God has given her great insight into what it means to be in a dark place. Her words do not resonate from a place of what she has heard but from what she has endured. She knows firsthand what it feels like to live in a dark and gloomy place, full of depression and anxiety. Refusing to die in her pain, she fought her way out, and now she is coming back to help pull others out of the darkness and encouraging them to step out from behind the shadows.

This book is a heart book that was meticulously written as she listened to the heart of God for instructions. Now is the perfect time for it to be released because of the tumultuous year we experienced due to the pandemic. Several individuals are broken, depressed, and lost in the dark. They are filled with fear, anxiety and need a reminder that God wants them to be free and live a life of joy and peace.

As an author and life coach, this book has shined a light on some dark areas in my life, and it has truly blessed my soul. After reading this powerful book, my prayer for everyone is that they, too, will be set free. I pray that they will read with their heart as they allow the words given to Johnnie Mae from our Heavenly Father to aid them out of their dark place.

Sylinda D.
Author/Life Coach
Atlanta, Georgia

Introduction

What is a shadow? A shadow is a dark area or shape produced by a body coming between light and a surface. A shadow is a dark shape that is formed when an object blocks a source of light. Shadows can also act as an action, like when you shadow or follow someone on the first day on a new job.

A shadow is something that is defined by the absence of light. To shadow someone means you will follow them around and observe what they are doing without disturbing them.

The face of a shadow could look like the following seven things. Let us view and define each one:

1. Shade: darkness
2. Darkness: Absence of light
3. Dimness: The state of being poorly illuminated

4. Gloom: Partial or total darkness
5. Murk Gloom, darkness; fog
6. Obscurity: The state of being unknown, inconspicuous, or unimportant
7. Umbrage: Shade or shadow

All the above words can be canonized and associated with the words gloom or unhappiness. These words have a dominating presence. Gloom postures the individual in a state of depression or despondency. What is despondency? It is of low spirits caused by loss of hope or courage.

A man that loses hope is like a ship without a sail or one that has no breath. What about depression? Depression is defined as a feeling of serve despondency and dejection I suggest to you today that these are all spirits designed to align one to inner darkness and turmoil.

Several people throughout the Bible have experienced depression, from Moses to King David. The word depression doesn't appear in scripture as it is used today except for Proverbs 12: 25, which offers a quick note of wisdom "Anxiety down the heart but a kind word cheers it up. The Hebrew word for weighted down is "shachah" which translates bow down or "depress."

The book of Psalms is rife with depression. Most of the Psalms was written by King David, who penned many of them in low moments. He wrote, so my Spirit grows faint within me, my heart within is dismay Psalms 143:4. A few passages over, he declares, answer me, Lord my Spirit fails. Do not hide your face from me, or I will be like those who go down to the pit *Psalms 143:7.*

Lamentations' whole book is a poetic expression of the Hebrews' deep unabashed deep depression after Jerusalem's fall, with no hope or redemption or resume. So, you see, behind the shadow, one would be simply existing. Yes, trapped and not operating at full potential.

Walk with the author as she paints a picture of the original intent of all things. *Genesis 1:1-6* declares in the beginning; God created the heavens and the earth, and the earth was without form and void, and darkness was upon the face of the deep, and the Spirit of God moved upon the face of the waters. And God said, Let there be light, and there was light. And God saw the light, and it was good, and God divided the light from the darkness. And God calls the light day and the darkness he called night and the evening, and the morning was the first day.

So, it is here we see the Creators original intent for his creation. As he divides and separates. What appeared as darkness soon became light.

It was in the dividing the separation was permitted to take place. The word divide simply means to separate or to separate into parts. To cut into distinct parts by incision. It was not until the Creator separated the darkness from the light, darkness dissipated. The ability to receive the cut will produce the unlocking for movement.

Behind the shadow lives a world full of possibilities. A world full of mobility. Mobility is defined as having the ability to move or to be moved freely and easily. You see, when one step from behind the shadow, freedom is express. You now become liberated. You exhibit the power to manifest the power or right to act, speak or think as one wants without hindrance or restraint. In freedom, you experience the estate of not being imprisoned or enslaved. Apostle Paul puts it like this in his letter to the Romans. "But now that you have been set free from sin and become slaves to

God, the benefits lead you to holiness, and the results are eternal life." *Romans 6:22*
He wrote a letter to Peter telling him we should live as free men but do not use freedom to cover up evil. We should live as servants of God. I Peter 4:16.

Socrates said, "to find yourself, think for yourself. President John F. Kennedy states the greatest history of a man's past, present, and future is the revolution of those determined to be free. Albert Camus, a French author, journalist, and philosopher, declared, "Freedom is nothing but a chance to be better."

Let us take the journey with the author as she shows us the pathway to living from behind the shadow.

Chapter 1

"How did We Get Here"

If one will position himself to come from behind the shadow to be in the forefront, he must examine himself. The purpose of the examination will keep the individual honest with himself. Self-examination is the best way to free oneself from every inclination of sabotage.

The Spirit of sabotage is to deliberately destroy, damage, or obstruct (something). Its face looks like the words listed below:

1. To Wreck: To bring to destruction, to break up
2. To Damage: To impair or bring to ruin
3. To Spoil: Damage, diminish or destroy the value or quality of
4. To Ruin: The physical destruction or disentigrati0n of something

5. To Undermine: To subvert or weaken insidiously or secretly. To weaken by degrees
6. To Vandalize: To deliberately destroy or damage

The Spirit of sabotage works with other spirits to take you to task, hamper you, hurt you, and purposefully subvert you. Subvert means to secretly try to ruin or destroy a system. To make something weaker or less effective, to overturn and overthrow the foundation and pervert and corrupt by undermining morals' allegiance or faith.

This Spirit operates as a strong demonic influence that drives people to abort the progress and success of divinely ordain projects, purposes, relationships, organizations, self-potential, and destinies. This Spirit is skillful and will use you as a pawn and a puppet on a string prohibiting you from detecting its hand upon you. So, you see, self-examination is like a key designed to unlock your feet for mobility.

How did we get behind the shadow? After the fall of mankind, both Adam and Eve were dressed and sent out of the garden. To the reader, even though there was a separation, good and evil still existed. As we review the fall of mankind, we also see an act of redemption that temporarily removed the shadow of darkness.

Adam and Eve were covered with a garment and driven out but graced to live in their dispensation. In this grace, their ability to walk in function was key to their method of survival. As they stepped out from the garden, they understood that darkness would ever be present, but the light of who they were could never be eliminated. The only way their status would be changed is if the enemy of their souls would whisper lies to them once again. These lies would allow Adam and Eve to be positioned to live in their past. One must understand and recognize that living in the past could become detrimental for the future. Come let us visit the text of scriptures

Genesis 3 and 4:1-2:

Now the serpent was craftier than any of the wild animals the LORD God had made. He said to the woman, "Did God really say, `You must not eat from any tree in the garden'?" The woman said to the serpent, "We may eat fruit from the trees in the garden, but God did say, `You must not eat fruit from the tree that is in the middle of the garden, and you must not touch it, or you will die.' "You will not surely die," the serpent said to the woman. "For God knows that when you eat of it, your eyes will be opened, and you will be like God, knowing good and evil." When the woman saw that the tree's fruit was good for food and pleasing to the eye and also desirable for gaining wisdom, she took some and ate it. She also gave some to her husband, who was with her, and he ate it. Then the eyes of both of them were opened, and they realized they were naked; so, they sewed fig leaves together and made coverings for themselves. The man and his wife heard the sound of the LORD God as He was walking in the garden in the cool of the day, and they hid from the LORD God among the trees of the garden. But the LORD God called to the man, "Where are you? "He answered, "I heard you in the garden, and I was afraid because I was naked; so, I hid. "And he said, "Who told you that you were naked? Have you eaten from the tree that I commanded you not to eat from? "The man said, "The woman you put here with me--she gave me some fruit from the tree, and I ate it. "Then the LORD God said to the woman, "What is this you have done?" The woman said, "The serpent deceived me, and I ate. "So, the LORD God said to the serpent, "Because you have done this, "Cursed are you above all the livestock and all the wild animals! You will crawl on your belly, and you will eat dust all the days of your life. And I will put enmity between you and the woman, and between your offspring and hers; he will crush your head, and you will strike his heel. "To the woman, he said, "I will greatly increase your pains in childbearing; with pain, you will give birth to children. Your desire will be for your husband, and he will rule over you. "To Adam, he said, "Because you listened to your wife and ate from the tree about which I commanded you, `You must not eat of it,' "Cursed is the ground because of you; through painful toil, you will eat of it all the days of your life. It will produce thorns and thistles for you, and you will eat the plants of the field. By the sweat of your brow, you will eat your food until you return to the ground since from it you were taken; for dust you are, and to dust, you will return. "Adam named his wife Eve because she would become the mother of all the living. The LORD God made garments of skin for Adam and his wife and clothed them. And the LORD God said, "The man has now become like one of us, knowing good and evil. He must not be allowed to reach out his hand and take from the tree of life and eat and live forever. So, the LORD God banished him from the Garden of Eden to work the ground from which he had been taken.

After he drove the man out, he placed on the east side of the Garden of Eden cherubim and a flaming sword flashing back and forth to guard the way to the tree of life.

Genesis 4:1-2

Adam laid with his wife Eve, and she became pregnant and give birth to Cain. She said, with the help of the Lord, I have brought forth a man. Later she gave birth to his brother Abel. Now Abel kept flocks, and Cain works the soil.

The seat of darkness will always try to dominate the seat of light. It will be up to the individual to take their rightful place. Stepping out in courage and dominating every sphere. Adam and Eve stood from behind the shadow and remember the word of the Lord. The women's seed would bruise the serpent's head and brought forth children standing in their identities as they stood from behind the shadow.

Chapter 2
Bound

Leaving *Genesis 3 and 4*, we find that humanity has a dual nature. Defining it, the author looks at both extremes of mankind. You might ask what are they? They are Spirit and Flesh. Let us put the two in perspective:

1) Spirit

2) Flesh

The Spirit is the non-physical part of a person. It is the immaterial intelligent or sentient part of a person. Which is the seat of emotions and character, the soul. I would like to call it the divine part of mankind. It is the God-man

When we speak of the flesh, we are not talking about the human body created by God. Paul references it as a code word for distortion that original sin introduced into human nature. The flesh twists and misdirects natural desires to make them destructive and degrading. It is what the flesh does, and that is sin.

The two are at war daily.

There is a constant struggle taking place in the life of every human being. To struggle is to make aggressive or violent efforts to get of restraint or constriction. To paint a clear picture, its face appears as the six words listed below. Come let us dig a little deeper by viewing the defined words listed:

1. Oppose: To disapprove of and to attempt to prevent, especially by argument
2. Contest: To engage competition to attain in
3. Fight: To take part in a violent struggle involving the exchange of physical blows or the use of
4. Conflict: A serious disagreement or argument
5. Endeavor: To try hard to do or achieve something
6. Encounter: Unexpectedly experience or be faced with (something difficult or hostile)

In other word's it means to contend with an adversary or opposing forces. What is an adversary? An adversary is one's opponent in a contest, conflict, or dispute. It is here we find the war begins. Galatians 5;19 declares the sinful nature wants to do evil, which is just the opposite of what the Spirit wants. And the Spirit gives us desires that are opposite of what sinful nature desires. These two forces are constantly fighting each other, so you are not free to carry out your own will. So, it is here we see the raging war. Yes, the struggle is real. This reality is for your identity.

Therefore, if the enemy of your soul could keep you bound and restricted,

you are already his pawn. Hidden behind the shadow, he locks you down with his truth. His truth declares you are bound to the lie of yesterday. So, with perverted truth, you never reach full potential.

It is here the author shows you the untold truth about perverted wisdom. Perverted wisdom is a painted picture of a lie with invisible chains that grips the ankles and locks one's feet into a stagnation place. Stagnation is defined as the state of not moving or flowing. It is a lack of activity, growth, or development.

Sounds like retardation to me. What is retardation? It is the action of delaying or slowing the progress or development of something.

We see as the scripture close's in chapter 3 and opens in Genesis 4 the power of the active word of God remembered. It wasn't until Adam and Eve remembered the prophecy that the women's seed would bruise the serpent's head. They walked in their identities and knew each other and brought forth sons, and their names were called Cain Able. In the shadow, they argued until they remember who they were called to dominate, so as they remember their Creator, they understood it was a must they participate in their deliverance.

Allowing God's word to penetrate their spirits, Adam and Eve's true identities surface back to the forefront, which allowed them to produce just as God commanded in the days of creation.

You see, living with perverted truth erases what God says and echo the voice of the deceiver louder. Pause with the author and allow her to ask you one question. Who have you allowed to whisper in your ears lately that cast a shadow before you?

It is imperative that we allow the father's words to drown out every word that is not aligned with the pattern of God's Divine path for our lives. To drown out, we simply mean to cancel out the assignment of any lie. What is a lie? It is an unspoken truth. Adam and Eve were able to move forward by canceling the words assigned by the enemy of their soul and clothing themselves in God's promises.

The Bible is filled with the promise of God. From Genesis to Revelations, we read of ordinary people receiving the promises of God. These promises are received by the highest be authority, which is God's word.

When God makes a promise to his people, it will come to pass. What is a promise? A promise is a covenant or declaration that one will do exactly, or something will happen just as pledged.

As the world becomes our garment, we step to the forefront, and an exchange takes place. What is an exchange? It is a transaction; it is an act of giving one thing and receiving another. It is the act or process of receiving one thing or another. That exchange is light for darkness.

Psalms 129:130 declares at the entrance of your word, giveth light, it giveth understanding to the simple.

So, the shadow of darkness fade. The word becomes a light unto one's feet and unto his pathway—birthing mobility for the future. Our God is a God of progression and mobility. We see from the beginning of creation how He gave us the example of movement. He painted a clear picture of stepping out and moving. He cleared darkness by separating the firmaments above and beneath. His progression gave us the first example of stepping out of darkness, and as he stepped out, the light was produced. The darkness he called night and the light he called day. The evening and the morning were the first day. So powerful, right? Visit Genesis 1and see this great example.

There is liberty that comes with movement. As you move, every restriction that once held you bound, and captive must release its grip.

I am reminded of a powerful story found in the Book of Joshua. After the death of Moses, his mentee Joshua was behind the shadow according to Joshua 1

Joshua was a hidden figure. Why because he was afraid to lead the people. The shadow was cast over him because he believes that he could not cross a people across the Jordan. The shadow made him question his ability to do and become. Take a journey with the author as she revisits Joshua's identity crisis behind the shadow.

Let us read the text:

Joshua 1 NIV

1 After the death of Moses, the servant of the Lord, the Lord said to Joshua son of Nun, Moses' aide: "Moses my servant is dead. Now then, you and all these people, get ready to cross the Jordan River into the land I am about to give to them—to the Israelites. I will give you every place where you set

your foot, as I promised Moses. Your territory will extend from the desert to Lebanon. The Euphrates—all the Hittite country—to the Mediterranean Sea in the West from the great river. No one will be able to stand against you all the days of your life. As I was with Moses, I will be with you; I will never leave you nor forsake you. 6 Be strong and courageous because you will lead these people to inherit the land, I swore to their ancestors to give them.

"Be strong and very courageous. Be careful to obey all the law my servant Moses gave you; do not turn from it to the right or to the left, that you may be successful wherever you go. Keep this Book of the Law always on your lips; meditate on it day and night so that you may be careful to do everything written in it. Then you will be prosperous and successful. Have I not commanded you? Be strong and courageous. Do not be afraid; do not be discouraged, for the Lord your God will be with you wherever you go."

So, Joshua ordered the officers of the people: "Go through the camp and tell the people, 'Get your provisions ready. Three days from now, you will cross the Jordan here to go in and take possession of the land the Lord your God is giving you for your own.'"

But to the Reubenites, the Gadites, and the half-tribe of Manasseh, Joshua said, "Remember the command that Moses the servant of the Lord gave you after he said, 'The Lord your God will give you rest by giving you this land.' Your wives, children, and livestock may stay in the land that Moses gave you east of the Jordan. Still, all your fighting men, ready for battle, must cross over ahead of your fellow Israelites. You are to help them until the Lord gives them rest, as he has done for you, and until they too have taken possession of the land the

Lord your God is giving them. After that, you may go back and occupy your own land, which Moses the servant of the Lord gave you east of the Jordan toward the sunrise."

Then they answered Joshua, "Whatever you have commanded us we will do, and wherever you send us, we will go. Just as we fully obeyed Moses, so we will obey you. Only may the Lord your God be with you as he was with Moses. Whoever rebels against your word and does not obey it will be put to death whatever you may command them. Only be strong and courageous.

Indeed, if one is going to come forth, freedom is a must. To be free means you are not in control or in the power of another. Able to act or be done as one wishes. Not or no longer in prison. It simply means to be released from captivity, confinement, or slavery.

The shadow had Joshua stuck. He was in training for leadership, but he stood behind the shadow when His mentor died. Full of grief, he forgot all that he was exposed to. The shadow made him forget the following:

- ✓ That he made it out of Egypt
- ✓ That he survived the plagues
- ✓ That he walked with God and was given the power to overcome
- ✓ That he was given instructions by a great prophet.
- ✓ That he walked through the red sea.
- ✓ That he participated in several miracles

How easy it was for him to forget what he experienced. Wow, he had experienced the miraculous. When a shadow appears, it brings darkness. This darkness can erase and distort the truth. The word of the Lord was given to him several times. Still, it was not until Joshua applied the promise that the shadow was eliminated and had good success. I would like to say the word of the Lord caused a paradigm shift to take place in his life. A paradigm is an example. It is a model or pattern.

When you change a paradigm, you are simply changing a mindset. A paradigm shift occurs when one paradigm loses its influence, and another takes over. True paradigm shifts represent drastic, sometimes uncomfortable changes.

To come out from behind the shadow, Joshua had to gird himself in the power of the promise. This postured him to no longer be bound. Becoming empowered created newfound freedom, and he stepped from behind the shadow and was no longer bound. He got up and crossed the people over the Jordan. When he stood up, even the waters around him stood up.

Just as the waters stood up for Joshua and the Israelites crossed over onto dry land, the author desires for the reader to know the miraculous is believing in the power of God's Word. The power of it does the shifting and the empowering. With empowerment comes dominion for mobility to come from behind the shadow. I once heard someone sing, "Where there is a shadow, God's light is somewhere around and, in that light, there is freedom.

Chapter 3
Chains Falling

The author opens with this quote from an unknown author. 'The chains that break you are the chains that make you". What is a chain? A chain is a flexible series of metal links used for fastening or securing objects and pulling or supporting loads. Chains consist of the circled that are linked together. There are no beginning and no end, just like everything eternal. We must note through centuries

, chains had fewer positive connotations. They became the symbols of imprisonment, slavery, oppression, and great pain.

Through the corridor of time, one can hear the clinking of chains now falling. Come with the author as she takes you down the corridor, hearing chains hitting the ground as liberty speaks loud and clear. With every step a conscious decision is made to break free from old systems, patterns, and cycles. What is a decision? A decision is a conclusion or resolution reached after consideration. It is a final judgment. One must note that when a decision is made, it not only affects the person who makes the decision but every one that is connected to that individual.

Allow the author to use an example regarding decision-making affecting a family. There is a family that has six siblings. One of the family members lost their job and has been afraid of losing everything. Therefore, he makes a terrible decision. He decides to deceive his family. The word deceives means you have caused someone to believe something that is not true, typically to gain some personal advantage.

In other words, it is to:

- Give a mistaken impression
- To Swindle
- To Defraud

- To Cheat
- To Mislead
- To Beguile
- To Entrap

It simply means you have lied. To the reader, please understand to tell one lie, you must prepare yourself to tell another. Why? Untold truth will never come out the same way the second time. What the reader must come to a grip with is one lie leads to another, always painting a different scenario

The deceiver is ashamed because he lost his employment. So daily, he gets up, gets dressed, eats breakfast, and exits out the door with the impression that he is working a 9-5. In shame

he makes a cover-up and allows the whispers of untruth to become louder. With untruth, he musters up enough courage to continue with this Spirit called deception. So, he plots a major heist. Committing an armed robbery never really counting the cost of telling a lie. Operating with this

Spirit cast a dark shadow that affected many areas of his life. Let us look at what was affected by his action:

1. His Family,
2. His Freedom
3. His Finances
4. His Mindset

How did the lie affect the above? Allow the author to explain. Let us review each scenario below:

1. Family

We are all attached to someone, and when we make a terrible choice, it can shift the dynamics of everyone's lifestyle. Robbing the bank removed the husband as the head of the household. This placed a burden on the wife. Positioning her to struggle to meet the financial needs of the family. The children are left fatherless. We all know that two are better than one.

Ecclesiastes 4:9-12 declares NIV That two are better than one because they have a good return for their labor: If either of them falls one can help the other up.

But pity anyone who falls and has no one to help them up. Also, if two lies down together, they will keep warm. But how can one keep warm alone? Though one may be overpowered, two can defend themselves. A cord of three strands is not quickly broken.

So, you see, two is better than one. From the beginning of creation, we find the structure of the family established. It was declared it was not good for man to be alone. So, the family was instituted. Therefore, we now see how two is better than one.

Genesis 1 declared it was not good for man to be alone, so God made man and woman, and here begins the family's institution. So, the two became one in the Spirit. Therefore, what is forgotten is what affects the one will affect the other because they are one by way of Spirit. We are family. The stigma of one's error is sometimes associated with the family. Why? Because humanity does not always see through the proper lenses. A man's sin is simply dressed on his personal shoulders and not another with the proper perspective. Being one of the family sometimes wear the shame, the stigma, and guilt of another person's error until they correctly see themselves as individuals and their uniqueness.

2.) Freedom

"Freedom is the oxygen of the soul," quote Moshe Dayan. Martin Luther King declared, "Let freedom ring from every mountainside." As a young teenager hearing my mother singing these words "I am free, praise the Lord I am free. No longer bound, no more chains holding me. My soul is resting; it's just a blessing. Praise the Lord hallelujah I'm free.

Today I understand she was free from all that once held her in captivity. What she was declaring in her atmosphere, nothing can hold me captive.

To be free is to have liberty. It is the power or right to act or speak or think as one wants without hindrance or restraints. It is the state of not being imprisoned. So, you see, when deception is present, the keys to the cell always await the cuffs.

Once deception is presented, freedom is immediately snatched away. The manifestation of a shadow of darkness is cast, and the cell is presented.

I am reminded of a story I read in the book of Genesis about a young man named Jacob. Jacob is a biblical hero who depicts the power and Grace of God to change and renew. He is most commonly known in the Bible for his cunning and deceitful ways, especially towards his twin brother

Esau. However, after losing to God in a wrestling match, Jacob received God's blessing and a new name. Before receiving the blessing, he lived a life full of deception. Come with the author and let us visit the text in *Genesis 27: 1- 46*.

When Isaac was old, and his eyes were so weak that he could no longer see, he called for Esau, his older son, and said to him, "My son."

"Here I am," he answered Isaac said, "I am now an old man and don't know the day of my death. Now then, get your equipment—your quiver and bow—and go out to the open country to hunt some wild game for me. Prepare me the kind of tasty food I like (and bring it to me to eat, so that I may give you my blessing before I die."

Now Rebekah was listening as Isaac spoke to his son Esau. When Esau left for the open country to hunt game and bring it back, Rebekah said to her son Jacob, "Look, I overheard your father say to your brother Esau, 'Bring me some game and prepare me some tasty food to eat, so that I may give you my blessing in the presence of the Lord before I die.' Now, my sons, listen carefully and do what I tell you: Go out to the flock and bring me two choice young goats, so I can prepare some tasty food for your father, just the way he likes it.

Then take it to your father to eat so that he may give you his blessing before he dies."

Jacob said to Rebekah, his mother, "But my brother Esau is a hairy man while I have smooth skin. What if my father touches me? I would appear to be tricking him and would bring down a curse on myself rather than a blessing."

His mother said to him, "My son, let the curse fall on me. Just do what I say, go and get them for me."

So, he went and got them and brought them to his mother, and she prepared some tasty food, just the way his father liked it. Then Rebekah took the best clothes of Esau, her older son, which she had in the house, and put them on her younger son Jacob. She also covered his hands and the smooth part of history's neck with the goatskins. Then she handed her son Jacob the tasty food. He went to his father and said, "My father.' "Yes, my son," he answered. "Who is it?"

Jacob said to his father, "I am Esau, your firstborn. I have done as you told me. Please sit up and eat some of my game so that you may give me your blessing."

Isaac asked his son, "How did you find it so quickly? My son "The Lord your God gave me success," he replied.

Then Isaac said to Jacob, "Come near so I can touch you, my son, to know whether you really are my son Esau or not." Jacob a too went close to his father Isaac, who touched him and said, "The voice is the voice of Jacob, but the hands are the hands of Esau." He did not recognize him, for his hands were hairy like those of his brother Esau; so, he proceeded to bless him. "Are you really my son Esau?" he asked.

"I am," he replied. Then he said, "My son, bring me some of your game to eat so that I may give you my blessing. "Jacob brought it to him, and he ate, and he brought some wine, and he drank. Then his father Isaac said to him, "Come here, my son, and kiss me."

So, he went to him and kissed him. When Isaac caught the smell of his clothes, he blessed him and said, "Ah, the smell of my son is like the smell of a field that the Lord has blessed.

May God give you heaven's dew and earth's richness – an abundance of grain and new wine. May nations serve you, and peoples bow down to you. Be Lord over your brothers and may the sons of your mother bow down to you.

May those who curse you be cursed and those who bless you be blessed." After Isaac finished blessing him, and Jacob had scarcely left his father's presence, his brother Esau came in from hunting. He, too, prepared some tasty food and brought it to his father. Then he said to him, "My father, please sit up and eat some of my game so that you may give me your blessing."

His father Isaac asked him, "Who are you?" I am your son," he answered, "your firstborn, Esau."
Isaac trembled violently and said, "Who was it, then, that hunted game and brought it to me? I ate it just before you came, and I blessed him—and indeed he will be blessed!"

When Esau heard his father's words, he burst out with a loud and bitter cry and said to his father, "Bless me—me too, my father!"
But he said, "Your brother came deceitfully and took your blessing."

Esau said, "Isn't he rightly named Jacob? This is the second time he has taken advantage of me: He took my birthright, and now he's taken my blessing!" Then he asked, "Haven't you reserved any blessing for me?"

Isaac answered Esau, "I have made him Lord over you and have made all his relatives his servants, and I have sustained him with grain and new wine. So, what can I possibly do for you, my son?" Esau said to his father, "Do you have only one blessing, my father? Bless me too, my father!" Then Esau wept aloud.

His father Isaac answered him, "Your dwelling will be away from the earth's richness, away from the dew of heaven above. You will live by the sword, and you will serve your brother.

But when you grow restless, you will throw his yoke from off your neck."
Esau held a grudge against Jacob because of the blessing his father had given him. He said to himself, "The days of mourning for my father are near; then I will kill my brother Jacob."

When Rebekah was told what her older son Esau had said, she sent for her younger son Jacob. She said to him, "Your brother Esau is planning to avenge himself by killing you. Now then, my son, do what I say: Flee at once to my brother Laban in Harran. Stay with him for a while until your brother's fury subsides. When your brother is no longer angry with you and forgets what you did to

him, I will send word for you to come back from there.
Why should I lose both of you in one day?"

Then Rebekah said to Isaac, "I'm disgusted with living because of these Hittite women. If Jacob takes a wife from among the women of this land, from Hittite women like these, my life will not be worth living."

After reading the above text with the author, you now get a glimpse of the Spirit of deception in operation. We see all four of the author pillars.

The story of Jacob and his brother is one full of the Spirit of deception. The story depicts the mother and the brother operating with this Spirit. This opens gateways, portals, and channels for other spirits to gain access.

Let us review the scenarios that happened when the Spirit of deception appears and show its effects in ways that are damaging. Below you will find the 4 ways:

1. **Family** - He had to leave his family, and he was left alone.

2. **Freedom** - He had to run for his life and live-in hiding. Imprisonment

3. **Financially** - He had to leave what was established for him and work double. Yes, extra hard, and he was underhanded. Yes, he was cheated for his labor.

4. **Mindset** - his thinking was always locked on escaping from his brother. How to overcome his deception. He was trapped in one mindset and required a paradigm shift.

Genesis 27:36 Jacob means he grasps the heel, a Hebrew idiom for he takes advantage of, or he deceives. So, you see, deception is a killer. This Spirit utterly kills and manipulates the path for anyone who makes a conscious decision to live within its walls.

A few chapters over, we find that as Jacob confronts this Spirit, we see a change taking place. As the pages turn, we now see the chains that once held Jacob and the family members hostage now lose the power of their grip. The chains that once click have now become the sound of freedom.

The clinking of chains has now ceased, and with change, we see that the shadow has lost its grip. Where there is a shadow, God's light is always around.

The author paints a clear picture of those who operate with the Spirit of deception. When operating with this Spirit, one paints the scenario of a man standing over his own coffin with his hands extended, ready to close the casket over himself.

Mary Hawthorn quote, "Deception may give us what we want for the present, but it will always take it away in the end."

Walter Scott indicated, "Oh what a tangled web we weave when we practice deceiving. "

After one break free, and the taste of liberty is presented darkness is dispelled, and the Spirit of deception is dismantled. Deceit now becomes truth, and truth becomes the keys that unlocked every chain. The author declares this truth "in freedom, the deceiver is now released from captivity and confinement, or slavery. You see, the person that operates in or with the Spirit of deception has literally become a slave to it. Controlled by it, they are puppets chained, and with each step, the sound of the chains gets louder.

Now that the keys are released, we find the individual ready to be mobilized. As we go over a few more chapters in the book of Genesis, we see how Jacob the deceiver stepped from behind the dark shadow, and his name was changed to Israel.

Believe me, it was not an overnight process. He wanted to March forward with this same Spirit until he had a battle and wrestled with an angel. He was comfortable being a deceiver until he met his match.

Let us visit the text with the author: *Genesis 32: 1-32*

Jacob also went on his way, and the angels of God met him. When Jacob saw them, he said, "This is the camp of God! So, he named that place Mahanaim.

Jacob sent messengers ahead of him to his brother Esau in the land of Seir, the country of Edom. He instructed them: "This is what you are to say to my Lord Esau: 'Your servant Jacob says, I have been staying with Laban and have remained there till now. I have cattle and donkeys, sheep and goats, male and female servants. Now I am sending this message to my Lord that I may find favor in your eyes."

When the messengers returned to Jacob, they said, "We went to your brother Esau, and now he is coming to meet you, and four hundred men are with him."

In great fear and distress, Jacob divided the people who were with him into two groups, and the flocks and herds and camels. He thought, "If Esau comes and attacks one group, the group that is left may escape."

Then Jacob prayed, "O God of my father Abraham, God of my father Isaac, Lord, you who said to me, 'Go back to your country and your relatives, and I will make you prosper, I am unworthy of all the kindness and faithfulness you have shown your servant. I had only my staff when I crossed this Jordan, but now I have become two camps. Save me, I pray, from my brother Esau's hand, for I am afraid he will come and attack me and the mothers with their children. But you have said, 'I will surely make you prosper and will make your descendants like the sand of the sea, which cannot be counted.'"

He spent the night there, and from what he had with him, he selected a gift for his brother Esau: two hundred female goats and twenty male goats, two hundred ewes and twenty rams, thirty female camels with their young, forty cows and ten bulls, and twenty female donkeys and ten male donkeys. He put them in the care of his servants, each herd by itself, and said to his servants, "Go ahead of me, and keep some space between the herds."

He instructed the one in the lead: "When my brother Esau meets you and asks, 'Who do you belong to, and where are you going, and who owns all these animals in front of you?' then you are to say, 'They belong to your servant Jacob. They are a gift sent to my Lord Esau, and he is coming behind us.'"

He also instructed the second, the third, and all the others who followed the herds: "You are to say the same thing to Esau when you meet him. And be sure to say, 'Your servant Jacob is coming behind us.'" For he thought, "I will pacify him with these gifts I am sending on ahead; later, when I see him, perhaps he will receive me." So
Jacob's gifts went on ahead of him, but he spent the night in the camp.

That night Jacob got up and took his two wives, his two female servants, and his eleven sons and crossed the ford of the Jabbok. After he had sent them across the stream, he sent over all his possessions. So, Jacob was left alone, and a man wrestled with him till daybreak. When the man saw that he could not overpower him, he touched the socket of Jacob's hip so that his hip was wrenched as he wrestled with the man. Then the man said, "Let me go, for it is daybreak."

But Jacob replied, "I will not let you go unless you bless me."

The man asked him, "What is your name?" "Jacob," he answered. Then the man said, "Your name will no longer be Jacob, but Israel because you have struggled with God and with humans and have overcome." Jacob said, "Please tell me your name." but he replied, "Why do you ask my name?" Then he blessed him there.

So, Jacob called the place Peniel, saying, "It is because I saw God face to face, and yet my life was spared." The sun rose above him as he passed Peniel, and he was limping because of his hip. Therefore, to this day, the Israelites do not eat the tendon attached to the socket of the hip,) because the socket of Jacob's hip was touched near the tendon.

After reading the above text, the author desires for the reader to see what absolute freedom looks like through a repented heart's eyes. No longer do we see or hear chains, but we see a paradigm shift. Keys are given as Jacob makes a conscious decision to release his will. We see the dismantling and dissipating of a spirit that ruled for many years. Making the decision to change opened the portal for liberty. With this opened portal, the keys released him to receive the following:

- Mobilization
- Clear Perception
- The name changes from Jacob to Israel
- Covenant relationship with God and man
- The Blessing

So, you see, it wasn't until Jacob let go of his will and way of deception he was mobilized to move freely in his true identity. With liberty, Jacob now Israel moves with keys freely in repentance to live in the original intent of God. With no more chains, we see two families coming together as one. With clear perception, the released victim becomes the original intent of God's mindset, the victor.

In closing, I found this quote by Rosa Luxemburg "Those who don't move don't notice their chains." I see the chains falling.

Chapter 4
Stepping from Behind the Shadow

"Each step you take reveals a new horizon." The author would like to differentiate the difference between the Shadow of the Almighty vs. The Shadow of Darkness. The Shadow of the Almighty in the presence of God. It is God always surrounding you. In his presence, all goods are yours. You are in His protective custody. This place allows you to be at peace in every circumstance. This place is filled will liberation. Casting no limitations or chains of entrapment.

As stated earlier, the Shadow of Darkness is a place of imprisonment, polarization, and no mobilization. It is in this place you lose all of your rights to walk in your full potential. It's a place where your true identity is hidden, and you are entrapped, and your mind becomes a battlefield between good and evil. It Is actually a playground. In this place, you are a prisoner by your own decision. The Shadow of Darkness serves as a prison with invisible bars holding each person in captivity when they were actually born to be free. With surrendered arms, you are at a standstill.

To the reader, the author desires for you to understand and remember that your temple (body) is the house the Ruach. Ruach in Hebrew, meaning the breath or Spirit of the living God. It is imperative to realize that great potential is housed within each person.

Evangelist McCall declares, "untapped potential is like a body without breath." So, you see a painted picture of this is a dead man walking. Reminded of a story in the old testament of a young mentee name Joshua. Joshua had a great mentor. His mentors' name was Moses. Joshua walked with Moses and saw many miracles. He witnesses the plagues and the deliverance of his people. He even walked through the Red Sea with his mentor, the Rod. His mentor died, and everything Joshua experienced, everything that was imparted temporarily, went out the window. A shadow of darkness locked him down. He was paralyzed and was not focus.

Come let us visit the text together:
Read *Joshua Chapter 1 - 8*

We see the word of the Lord came several times, and it wasn't until Joshua made a conscious decision to get up, he was mobilized to his full potential, and he received liberty to:

- Obtain good success
- Lead Israel
- Walls of Jericho fell
- Crossed the families over the Jordan.
- Circumcision and Passover at Gilgal
- Remove the accursed item - defeat the enemy

We were never born to sit still. From the womb, a great movement took place. The egg had to swim to the seed, and even in the womb, activity was taking place. The embryo swims and created movement simply to communicate with its mother. I am here.

We were formed and created with great potential. We have the DNA of heaven, and the fight is for our existence. The author wants the reader to understand that they are fully loaded with potential and purpose.

Joshua shows us an excellent example of standing behind a shadow and not tapping into our true identity. You were created with and in for the purpose. In my closing, remember you were born to dominate. When he created you, he gave you his breath, and he declares you have been given the power to dominate, subdue and rule. Genesis 1: 29-32 He declared be fruitful, increase in number and dominate the earth. He gave you his breath to rule and reign. You are empowered to see yourself as the father sees you, which is likened unto his goodness. Yes, his image. Lap Tzu declared, "A journey of a thousand miles must begin with one single step."

It is my prayer you walk out your full potential as you stand in your Godly confidence

Prayer of Liberation

Yahweh,

Thank you for allowing us to enter into your courts, and with thanksgiving, we give you praise. It is in praise we find the path that you designed for the worshipper.

Father, as we stand under your opened heaven, we decree we now hide under your shadow. It is in this dwelling place we have found a hiding place. We decree that our feet are unlocked for purpose as we acknowledge you in all our ways.

Thank you, Father, for the keys that have been released to remove every shadow that comes to invade the place you called our hands to plow. We decree and declare our feet stand on the high place, and you are governing our every move as we, your people, dwell in your presence.

As we lift you high, it is declared your word now has become a lamp unto our feet, and a light unto our pathway. We say no to the enemy and decree he has no entrance. As you reveal yourself, as I am, strategies and downloads will be released for forwarding progression.

We now eliminate and remove every opposing distraction that serves as a hindrance to our God-given purpose. Be lifted as we are awakened and remain from behind the shadow.

We declare illumination comes by way of Revelation as we announce you as Yahweh in our lives. No darkness, no stagnation, and no parallelization in Jesus Christ's name. As we remain out from behind the shadow
your glorious light will illuminate men that are cloth in darkness.

We humble ourselves that you may heal the land as Jehovah Gibhor. Now Father, order our steps in your word and in this world.

Amen

Reference Page

Bible Gateway

- KJV
- Message
- NIV

Goodnet - quotes of freedom

Rosa Luxemburg quotes

https://www.christianity.com/wiki/bible/what-are-god-s-promises-in-the-bible.html

Wikipedia Dictionary

Dictionary.com

Christian Answers.com

Matthew Henry Commentary

Dr. Cindy Trimm - YouTube Pray Rules of Engagement

Author's Bio

Johnnie Mae McCall is an anointed multi-gifted inspirational, motivational, and seminar speaker. She is the Founder and CEO of the Embrace of the Father Ministry. This ministry provides hope for the hopeless and embraces and empowers many to walk in a purpose-driven life. She is the author of the Embrace of the Father, and Healing is the Children's Bread. She is a member of the New Jersey Strategic Network of Intercessors.

Johnnie Mae is submitted under the Leadership of Apostle Cierra LaShaun Jones. He is a member of The United Kingdom Global Impact Alliance Prophetic Conservatory. Under this leadership, she attends the School of the Prophets. UK

Conservatory Alliance and sit under the Mantel and Mentorship Program.

Johnnie Mae has obtained her Bachelor Associates Degree and master's degree in Theology from the United Christian Bible School and is accredited from Jameson Christian College, Where Dr. James P. Williams serves as Dean.

She has worked for over 36 years as a Business Administrator for Goldman Sachs & Co. Johnnie is very dedicated to hospital, prison, and street ministry. She is one of 7 siblings. You will always hear her declare, "We must become the literal embrace from above. Just as the Father Embraced us, we should embrace others.

Contact Information

You can follow me on my social media outlets

FB @ johnnie.mccall

or you can email me at:

2018jmae@gmail.com

www.ingramcontent.com/pod-product-compliance
Lightning Source LLC
LaVergne TN
LVHW020657100826
845148LV00012B/2538